kickstart your life with NLP

Paul Jenner

Hodder Education

338 Euston Road, London NW1 3BH.

Hodder Education is an Hachette UK company

First published in UK 2011 by Hodder Education

Copyright © 2011 Paul Jenner

The moral rights of the author have been asserted

Database right Hodder Education (makers)

All rights reserved. No part of this publication may be reproduced, stored in a retrieval system or transmitted in any form or by any means, electronic, mechanical, photocopying, recording or otherwise, without the prior permission in writing of Hodder Education, or as expressly permitted by law, or under terms agreed with the appropriate reprographic rights organization. Enquiries concerning reproduction outside the scope of the above should be sent to the Rights Department, Hodder Education, at the address above.

You must not circulate this book in any other binding or cover and you must impose this same condition on any acquirer.

British Library Cataloguing in Publication Data: a catalogue record for this title is available from the British Library.

10 9 8 7 6 5 4 3 2 1

The publisher has used its best endeavours to ensure that any website addresses referred to in this book are correct and active at the time of going to press. However, the publisher and the author have no responsibility for the websites and can make no guarantee that a site will remain live or that the content will remain relevant, decent or appropriate.

The publisher has made every effort to mark as such all words which it believes to be trademarks. The publisher should also like to make it clear that the presence of a word in the book, whether marked or unmarked, in no way affects its legal status as a trademark.

Every reasonable effort has been made by the publisher to trace the copyright holders of material in this book. Any errors or omissions should be notified in writing to the publisher, who will endeavour to rectify the situation for any reprints and future editions.

Hachette UK's policy is to use papers that are natural, renewable and recyclable products and made from wood grown in sustainable forests. The logging and manufacturing processes are expected to conform to the environmental regulations of the country of origin.

www.hoddereducation.co.uk

Typeset by Cenveo Publisher Services.

Printed in Great Britain by CPI Cox & Wyman, Reading.

Contents

1	NLP – the basics	2
2	Transform your past	20
3	Transform your learning abilities	32
4	Transform your inner voice	38
5	Transform your success	48
6	Transform your health	58
7	Transform your powers of persuasion	64
8	Transform your love life	80

1

NLP – the basics

NLP stands for Neuro-Linguistic Programming, developed from the 1970s onwards by John Grinder and Richard Bandler. Yes, it's quite a mouthful. And somewhat daunting. Which is why most people say simply, 'NLP'. Various definitions of NLP have been put forward, but the fact is that NLP is *not* a single discipline so much as a collection of quite different techniques. So, in reality, no definition is possible. Nor is there a widely accepted definition of what NLP *does*. So I'm going to give you my own:

> *NLP is a collection of techniques that can rapidly put you in control of your mind.*

In this first chapter I'll give you an overview of the most popular techniques and in subsequent chapters we'll look at them in more detail.

Behind NLP is the observation that the things you experience must be organized in your mind in some structured way. Once you understand the structure, you can better control your mind. Once you're in control of your mind, you're in control of your body and your behaviour. You're in control of your life. You have more choices.

Modelling

We'll start with modelling, because that's how the whole NLP adventure began back in the early 1970s. At that time John Grinder was teaching at the University of California Santa Cruz and Bandler was a fourth-year undergraduate. In the book *Whispering in the Wind*, Grinder recounts how every week Bandler would knock on his door and invite him to attend a group that he, Bandler, was leading in Gestalt Therapy (a style of psychotherapy that stresses the present moment). Each time Grinder would decline, saying he didn't need therapy. It was only after a few weeks that Bandler explained he actually wanted Grinder to 'figure out how to describe' what Bandler and his friend Frank Pucelik were doing as therapists. Bandler was having a lot of success and, according to Grinder, bringing about rapid and profound changes in clients, but he didn't know how to pass on his skills to others.

Grinder, who had a doctorate in transformational linguistics, was intrigued enough to attend the group and was immediately hooked. Grinder and Bandler's collaboration led not only to a detailed analysis of the methods of Fritz Perls (the father of Gestalt Therapy) as employed by Bandler and Pucelik, but also later those of the 'Family Therapist' Virginia Satir. As a result they created the so-called Meta Model and published it in the first NLP book, *The Structure of Magic, Volume 1*.

> ### Jargon buster – meta
>
> The prefix **'meta'** crops up quite a lot in NLP, to mean 'going beyond'. As Bandler and Grinder wrote, '... each of these wizards (Perls and Satir) has a map or model for changing their clients' models of the world...'. Meta also implies change or transcendence. The Meta Model is all about challenging superficial and imprecise ways of talking (and therefore thinking) so as to provoke people into change.

What would you say if you, as an aspiring musician, were watching the cellist Yo Yo Ma? I'll tell you. *I could never do that*.

Well, NLP doesn't accept that you could never do *that*. NLP believes you can do anything anybody else can do, whether it involves a physical skill, a mental skill or an emotional skill. That's one of NLP's basic beliefs or 'presuppositions'.

> ### Jargon buster – presupposition
>
> The NLP **presuppositions** are a set of principles which underpin the whole NLP approach and which it's recommended you should live by. NLP is still developing and new presuppositions are being added, but most coaches teach between 10 and 20 presuppositions. Here's something rather special about them: they're not necessarily 'true'. In fact, as you'll see, there are other things in NLP that aren't necessarily 'true'. The key thing is that the presuppositions – and everything else in NLP – should be *useful*. They should improve your life.

Here's a presupposition that relates to modelling:

 If one person can do something, anyone can learn to do it.

No, of course it's not literally true in every case. Some people start out with advantages that others do not have. But as a guiding principle it should be a crucial part of your outlook. Once you stop setting limits on what you think you can achieve then you can achieve unlimited things.

1 NLP – the basics

How? That's the next question, isn't it? One answer would be to copy people who have already succeeded. Unlike ordinary copying, modelling starts out as an intuitive process. It's important that to begin with you don't ask any questions either internally or out loud. One of the reasons is that the people you're modelling *may not know themselves how they achieve their results*. They may *think* they know. But they could be wrong.

We'll be returning to modelling in detail later. For now, here's a little exercise to give you a flavour of the intuitive approach.

Watch part of a film featuring an actor who has a very identifiable style – but don't try to describe anything about the actor in words, either out loud or inside your head. Simply *absorb* the actor by watching the clip again and again and again. Then have a go at mimicking the actor – the style of clothing, the voice, the delivery, the eyes, the way of moving and particularly (this is very important) the tiny little gestures and shifts that in NLP are known as micro-movements.

The Milton Model

For many years, Milton H Erickson (1901–80) was the most famous hypnotherapist in the USA. Once Grinder and Bandler had honed their modelling skills on the techniques of Perls and Satir, he was an obvious target for them.

According to John Grinder's account, given in *Whispering in the Wind*, he and Richard Bandler effectively used Erickson's own hypnotic techniques to persuade the famous hypnotist to see them at a time when he was 'sequestered' with his three closest students and not receiving visitors. Using a book called *Advanced Techniques of Hypnosis and Therapy* (a compilation of Erickson's articles edited by Jay Haley), they learned several techniques of trance induction and tried them out on one another. They then extracted what they thought worked best and compiled a little speech incorporating variations on two 'embedded commands', which were 'Make time now' and 'See us now'.

> ### Jargon buster – embedded commands
>
> **Embedded commands** are words or phrases that are contained within sentences and which, although unnoticed by the conscious mind, will be picked up by the unconscious as long as they're spoken skilfully. One way of drawing the attention of the unconscious to these embedded words is to lower the voice when speaking them. Try reading out the following sentences, lowering your voice for the words in italics:
>
> ***You can** learn what they did to *be successful*.*
> ***You can** agree it's healthier to *be a non-smoker*.*

Grinder and Bandler then tossed a coin and Grinder won the task of placing the phone call to Erickson. For two and a half minutes he ran through the induction that had been rehearsed, his voice gradually getting slower and slower and 'simply finally stopping'.

There was then half a minute's silence after which Erickson said, 'You boys come over here immediately'.

There were several important outcomes. Firstly, Grinder and Bandler advanced their modelling skills. Secondly, they were inspired to set about developing simple techniques that could, in some instances, replicate Erickson's results by means of clever visualizations (see below). Thirdly, they identified the key patterns of speech that Erickson used to achieve his remarkable results. These became known as the 'Milton Model' and were detailed in the two-volume work *Patterns of the Hypnotic Techniques of Milton H Erickson*, published in 1975 and 1977.

The essence of the Milton Model is that it's often 'artfully vague'. That was the phrase used by Bandler and Grinder in their book. In other words, rather than give a direct instruction ('You will do this', 'You will not do that') the Milton Model plants an idea. This seems to be the way the unconscious works best.

Talk to unconscious

Stories and quotes

When we order people to do things, nag, or even ask quite pleasantly, we're likely to encounter varying degrees of resistance. Most people don't like being told what to do. On the other hand, if we tell a story that subtly illustrates the point we're trying to make, then the other person's unconscious extracts the meaning from it. The effect can be quite profound, because when you have to work out something for yourself the solution comes like a revelation and you remember it better than if you'd been told directly.

Quotes work a little bit like stories. Rather than give a direct instruction yourself – which might create resistance – you instead quote another person, for example: 'As my headmaster used to say, "If a thing's worth doing, it's worth doing badly."'; 'I always remember my grandfather saying to me, "Drink is a weakness."'

Quote someone else

Presuppositions

In this context, a presupposition is a way of speaking in which you take certain things for granted, such as that the other person is going to do what you want. Let's say you're a car salesman. Rather than ask, 'Would you like to buy this car?' you instead ask, 'Do you want to take delivery at once or would you prefer to wait until next month?' By presupposing that you've made the sale, you put the customer in the position of having to oppose your will in order to get out of buying the car. Some people find that hard to do. This kind of presupposition is known as a 'double bind'.

Pacing and leading

Pacing and leading are standard techniques in hypnosis but they can also be used in everyday life.

> ### Jargon buster – pacing and leading
> **Pacing** means feeding someone's experience back to them, either by copying their body language, or by stating it ('your eyes are closing'), or both.
>
> **Leading** – which follows successful pacing – means guiding someone towards what you want them to do or feel.

When you feed someone's experience back to them, you establish both rapport and trust because the other person knows that everything you say is true. Pacing, done the right way, can also bring on an altered state of consciousness. The hypnotic technique has become well known, for example: 'You're sitting comfortably in that armchair, your hands resting lightly on your knees, your head against a cushion…'. However, verbal pacing in normal life would have to be a lot more ingenious, for example: 'Fred Bloggs, are you going to sit there in that armchair, with that grin on your face, telling me…'.

Cause and effect

This device links two separate statements. The first statement is known to be true and therefore it is more likely that the second statement will also be accepted as true, for example: 'This vehicle has an air-cooled engine and is the most reliable for desert use.' In this example the person being addressed knows the vehicle does, indeed, have an air-cooled engine and believes that, *because of that*, it's reliable in the desert, even though the speaker hasn't actually said so.

Phrasing

Most of the time, Erickson spoke in a soft, gentle, warm and considerate manner, employing a very unusual and very particular way of spacing his words and phrases.

To actually hear Erickson speaking go to www.youtube.com and enter 'Milton H Erickson' in the search facility.

Self-hypnosis

Erickson sometimes taught clients how to put themselves into trance so they could continue certain aspects of treatment at home. The method I'm about to describe now is, however, attributed not to Erickson but to his wife Betty, who was herself a hypnotist.

Jargon buster – ecology check

When you reprogram your unconscious mind there may be unforeseen consequences – not only for you but also for everyone around you. Carrying out an **ecology check** involves investigating all the possible ramifications before going ahead. The key questions are:

What will happen if I succeed in making this change?
What won't happen if I succeed in making this change?
What will happen if I don't succeed in making this change?
What won't happen if I don't succeed in making this change?

Have a go

Step 1: Get yourself comfortable in a place you won't be disturbed.

Step 2: Decide the length of time you wish to spend in self-hypnosis. So, having got comfortable, you should say something like this: 'I am now going to hypnotize myself for ten minutes.'

Step 3: This is a key step because it's where you state the purpose of your hypnosis. Something along these lines will do fine: 'I am entering into a state of self-hypnosis so that I can hand over to my unconscious mind the task of…'

Step 4: State how you want to feel when you come out of your trance.

SELF TRANCE V Good ex

Step 5: This is the actual process of self-hypnosis. Basically you're going to engage your three main representational systems in turn to bring the trance about. In the first part of the process you will be noting things you can actually see, hear and feel *in the room where you are*. In the second part you will be noting things you can see, hear and feel *in an imaginary scene*.

In this process some people talk to themselves internally, but I recommend that *you say everything out loud*.

a From your comfortable position, look at some small thing in the room in front of you and say out loud what you are looking at. Choose things you can see without moving your head. For example, 'I am looking at the door handle.' Then, without rushing, focus on another small item. For example, 'I am now looking at a glass of water on the table.' Then move on to a third item. For example, 'I am looking at the light switch.' When you have your three visual references, move on to b).

b Switch attention to sounds and, in the same way, note one after another until you have three, each time saying out loud what you're hearing. Then move on to c).

c Note things that you can feel with your body. For example, you might say, 'I can feel the seat pressing against my buttocks.' When you have your three, move on.

d Now repeat steps a) to c) but with only two items for each sense: two images, two sounds and two feelings. They must be different *from the ones you used before*. Speak a little more slowly.

e Again repeat steps a) to c) but with only one item per sense: one image, one sound and one feeling. Again, they must be different *from any that have gone before*. Speak even more slowly.

1 NLP – the basics

f Close your eyes (if they're not already closed) and think of a scene. Any scene will do. It could be the first thing that comes into your head.

g Using this imagined scene, go through the same process you already used for the real scene, but beginning with just one example of each of the three senses: one image, one sound and one feeling. When you've done that, increase to two examples and then three. (Three is usually enough, but if you've stipulated a lengthy session you may need to continue with your fantasy scene by going on to name four images, sounds and feelings, or five or even more.) Remember, each example must be *different*. You'll probably find you're automatically speaking very slowly now but if not, make a point of *slowing your voice down more and more*.

h After the allotted time, you should begin to come out of trance automatically. But it may help to announce, 'I'll count to three and when I reach three I'll be (whatever you said in Step 4).' Don't worry about getting 'stuck' in a trance. That won't happen. You may feel a little woozy for a while. If so, don't drive a car or do anything demanding until you're sure you're okay to do so.

Visualization

NLP uses a great deal of visualization, so it's a skill that, unless you're already very good at it, you'll need to practise. Strictly speaking, the word 'visualization' refers only to 'seeing' images in your 'mind's eye' (that's to say, recalling memories or creating fantasies), but I'm using the term to include things you can imagine hearing and feeling as well. Once you've created your 'internal cinema', you're then going to be manipulating what NLP calls 'submodalities' in various ways.

> ### Jargon buster – submodalities
>
> Later I'll be asking you to make the images you've visualized brighter or darker, bigger or smaller, closer or further away, and so on; to make sounds louder or quieter; to make sensations stronger or weaker. In the jargon of NLP, these kinds of qualities, possessed by internal images, sounds and feelings, are known as **submodalities**.

Using submodalities

When we're afraid of things we tend to imagine them *big*. For example, if you're afraid of dogs, when you think about them you probably have a dog's face completely filling your 'screen', its huge fangs bared and seeming to be the size of ice picks. When you think of somewhere you don't want to go – perhaps a hospital – you probably have an image that's dreary and colourless. Perhaps the weight of the building bears down on you and you can even smell it. And what happens when you think of something nice? Possibly the colours are warm and vivid.

The concept behind NLP is that you can turn all this back to front. That is, instead of allowing the way you feel to create the submodalities, you deliberately create the submodalities that will make you feel the way you would prefer to be. In other words, instead of seeing the dog full screen you reduce the size. Instead of the hospital being drab, you paint it in vibrant colours.

Manipulating images is a big part of NLP, so the more you practise the more effective you'll be. Don't worry if you can't actually see an image very clearly or for very long. That's how it is for most people.

Swishing

Swishing is a famous NLP visualization technique. Essentially it means quickly swapping one image for another so that the submodalities from the first image become transposed to the second image. We'll be seeing how this works later in the book.

Spinning

Here's a question. When you're visualizing something and feeling a particular emotion, *where* in your body do you feel it? And does it *move*? Does it *spin*?

Try holding your hand out in front of you, or a little to the side, as you talk about a subject and see how it spontaneously moves. It may be better to have someone watch you so you don't have to think about your hand but just let it behave naturally. You may find that your hand moves as if it's spinning something. In that case, note which way it moves when you're talking about something positive and how it moves when you're talking about something negative. In all probability, the two will be different.

Having identified the phenomenon of spinning, you can now set about controlling it and, by so doing, help to control and direct your emotions. If you go faster you intensify the feeling. If you go slower you reduce it. And, of course, you can try reversing the direction to create the opposite feeling.

Interpersonal skills

I'm using the heading of 'interpersonal skills' to lump together several important NLP techniques. Many of these also derive from the work of Milton Erickson, who believed that in order to be able to influence someone, he first needed to establish rapport.

Try to establish rapport with someone you've just met in the following ways.

1 By matching and mirroring, that is, subtly copying their body language.

Jargon buster – matching and mirroring

Matching is approximating someone else's body language.
Mirroring means so precisely copying someone else as to seem like a mirror image.

For example: if the other person reclines in a very casual way, you do the same. If they rest their chin on their hands, you do the same. And so on.

2 By subtly copying their way of expressing themselves. In particular, watch out to see if they have a primary representational system, which may be visual, auditory or kinaesthetic and, if so, employ the same kind of language.

Jargon buster – primary representational system

The **primary representational system** is the preferred way that a person internally experiences or relives something. For many people the primary experience is visual, but others 'think' first in sounds or feelings. A few might lean towards taste and smell – and many more will where food is concerned. The clue is given by the language people use, for example: 'At a *glance* it all looks pretty *clear*'; 'It all *sounds* good to me so I'll get *tuned in*'; 'I'm *feeling lukewarm* about this but let's keep in *touch*'.

3 By repeating what someone has said, before introducing an idea of your own. For example: 'So you're saying we should go somewhere different this year and try new things, such as having a holiday in Morocco. That's a great idea. What about diving in the Caribbean?'

All the time you're doing these things you need to calibrate.

Jargon buster – calibrating

Calibrating means observing someone's body language very closely and relating it to his or her emotional state. For example, you would note tone of voice, skin colour, posture, gestures, micro-movements and so on.

1 NLP – the basics

If your calibration suggests you're not having the effect you want then you'll obviously have to vary your techniques. (See the presupposition below: *If what you are doing isn't working, do something else.*)

Presuppositions

Before we leave this discussion on NLP basics we need to look at one last area, the NLP presuppositions. We've already met one of them in the discussion on modelling. Just to remind you, it was:

* If one person can do something, anyone can learn to do it.
* Here are the other main ones:
* The map is not the territory.
* Everyone lives in their own unique model of the world.
* Experience has a structure.
* People already have all the resources they need.
* The mind and body are parts of the same system.
* You cannot *not* communicate.
* The meaning of your communication is the response you get.
* Underlying every behaviour is a positive intention.
* People are always making the best choices available to them.
* If what you are doing isn't working, do something else.
* There's no such thing a failure, only feedback.
* People work perfectly.
* The most flexible people have the greatest chance of getting what they want.
* Choice is better than no choice.
* So let's take a look.

The map is not the territory

Obviously, a printed map is a representation of reality and not the actual ground itself. We all realize that. Yet most of us probably *do* believe that our 'internal maps' of the world are an accurate reflection of the way the world really is. But they're not. They're simply interpretations. Bandler and Grinder certainly weren't the first to make this observation. The actual presupposition is usually attributed to Alfred Korzybski (1879–1950) but the idea itself goes back a long way.

None of us want to feel we live in a fantasy world. We prefer to believe that we see the world as it really is. But, in fact, a fantasy is closer to the truth. Once you accept that idea, so the whole point of visualization becomes so much more obvious.

Everyone lives in their own unique model of the world

Now that we know these internal maps are merely interpretations, we can see that everyone's will be slightly different. Ask six people for an assessment of a politician, a policy, a meal or a book and you'll get six different answers.

Experience has a structure

The idea of this is that the information coming from our senses is encoded in a systematic way in our brains, just as computers also have a special way of storing data.

People already have all the resources they need

This is linked with the previous presupposition and was an important part of Erickson's philosophy. It doesn't mean that you already know how to play a violin but that you already have within you the building blocks – the mental structures, the reasoning powers, the emotions, the experiences and so on – that will allow you to solve your own problems and achieve what you want.

The mind and body are parts of the same system

When you think about something that's depressing, you probably drop your shoulders and let your head hang down – your mind affects your body. But if you now go out for an invigorating jog in the sunshine you'll probably feel more optimistic – your body affects your mind. NLP effectively sees the mind as being present not solely in the brain, but throughout the body.

You cannot *not* communicate

It's very important to realize that we're all communicating all the time, whether we intend to or not. Even silence is a kind of communication.

The meaning of your communication is the response you get

Most of us sometimes feel frustrated, irritable and even angry when someone, as we see it, misinterprets what we've said. But everyone's 'mental map' is slightly different and the way to judge the effectiveness of your communication is not by what you meant, but by what the other person understood.

Underlying every behaviour is a positive intention

Sometimes it can be very hard to understand other people and why they do the things they do. This simple concept is the key. In their own minds, people are always trying to do something positive.

People are always making the best choices available to them

This presupposition, closely related to the previous one, says that the choices people make seem to them the best available options at the time.

If what you are doing isn't working, do something else

Some versions of this presupposition add the words 'Do anything else'; anything else must be better than something

18   kickstart your life with NLP

that doesn't work. As Richard Bandler says, there are things that can seem like great ideas but if they don't actually work then you have to throw them out along with the square wheels.

There's no such thing as failure, only feedback

The NLP outlook is that we should all behave like infants who seem to have no sense of failure. They simply keep trying and trying – to crawl, to walk, to speak – until they succeed.

People work perfectly

Self-esteem is very important in NLP, which always aims to see people in a positive way. Someone who spends a lot of time lying around doing nothing would be seen as an expert in relaxation.

The most flexible people have the greatest chance of getting what they want

Look around in nature. The creatures that are the most adaptable are the most numerous and successful. If, like a panda, you insist on eating a special kind of bamboo and nothing else, then you're in danger of extinction.

Choice is better than no choice

If you always react in the same negative way to a certain kind of situation then, effectively, you have no choice.

We'll be encountering these presuppositions in various contexts as we move through the book. But they also make useful sayings that you can repeat to yourself in the manner of affirmations. For example, when you doubt your ability to do something you can repeat: 'I have all the resources I need' or, 'Other people can do this so I can learn to do it.'

1 NLP – the basics

2
transform your past

When you look back on your life so far, it probably appears to tell a story. Everything seems to lead, step by step, to where you are now. If you're happy with all of those past steps, all well and good. But most of us have things in our pasts that bother us.

Just as the present can seem to be like a stop on an unpleasant railway line from the past, so the future may look to be nothing more than an extension of the same trajectory. But it doesn't have to be that way. We can go back and change those steps. We can change that trajectory. In doing so we can make you feel better right now and give you a new future.

I should point out straight away that NLP isn't, in fact, very much concerned with the past. Not, that is, in the sense of delving back into your childhood to discover what events, traumatic or otherwise, have made you the person you are today. The approach is completely different from those kinds of therapies in which you might spend months or even years trying to uncover the incidents that have shaped your outlook. As Richard Bandler puts it, he doesn't need to understand *how* you became the way you are, he only needs to understand how you *keep* being that way. As he's fond of observing, the great thing about the past is that it's over.

When you tell someone else about your past, no matter how honest you think you're being, you can't do anything other than provide them with a distortion. Someone else, looking at your life so far, might select quite different facts as being more truly representative.

So let's look afresh at your personal history right now. Let's deselect any past events that are bothering you and let's, as it were, replace them with memories that are more positive. I emphasize that in this exercise we're not going to be altering any facts, so you don't have to be concerned about 'lying' to yourself or anybody else.

The first thing we need to do is discover your timelines.

> ### Jargon buster – timelines
>
> The way you code the pictures, smells, sounds, feelings and tastes from the past, as well as those you anticipate in the future, is known in NLP as a **timeline**.

The way to discover your timeline is to think of something neutral that you've done quite often and will continue to do in the future. That's to say, a regular activity that doesn't arouse strong feelings one way or the other. It could be cleaning your teeth, eating breakfast or going to the cinema, for example.

Think of an occasion when you did that thing very recently, when you did it a month ago, a year ago, two years ago and five years ago. Then imagine doing it in the future, next week, next month, next year, in two years and in five years. Now put each of those scenes into a small picture frame or onto a playing card and imagine them all at once.

Here's the key question. How are those little pictures arranged in your mind's eye? Do you see them scattered randomly all about or do you order them in some way? Most likely you order them, either according to 'through time' or 'in time'.

Jargon buster – 'through time' and 'in time'

- You have the pictures arranged in a straight line running across your vision with the oldest memories on the extreme left and the distant future on your extreme right. In NLP jargon, this is known as **'through time'**.
- You have the pictures arranged in front of you in a V-shape, with the oldest memories on the left at the far end of one limb of the V and the distant future on your right at the far end of the other limb of the V. In this case the present is represented at the point of the V, right in front of your face. This is also known as **'through time'**.
- Your timeline is straight, with your memories behind you and your future in front of you. In NLP jargon this is known as **'in time'**.

Learning to forget

Generally speaking, we forget as time passes. Everything becomes less vivid and less able to impact on our emotions. But, of course, there are exceptions. The elderly often remember childhood incidents more accurately than things that happened a week ago. And when it comes to traumatic events, we relive those experiences as if they were happening right now.

In effect, we repeatedly take them out of the timeline and replace them in today's position, right in front of our faces. As a result their impact never lessens. This is a lovely thing to do with nice memories but the worst possible thing with bad ones.

What we're going to do now is reverse the process. We're going to take unpleasant memories and move them further away. That's to say, we're going to take them out of sequence.

Let's say you have a painful memory that won't leave you alone. In that case, what you need to do is move it to the farthest end of your timeline.

Step 1: Compare the submodalities of recent and distant memories. (Submodalities are qualities – if you've forgotten about them, refer back to Chapter 1.)

Step 2: Envisage your timeline and find the memory on it.

Step 3: Lift out that memory, like removing one card from a card file.

Step 4: Now begin changing the qualities of the experience from those of a recent event to those of an event from the distant past. It may help to exaggerate the submodalities that make the experience seem very old. At the same time, steadily move the memory to the *far end* of your timeline of the past. In other words, if you're 'through time' you'll be pushing the memory away to your left. Naturally, the picture will become smaller and smaller and less and less distinct.

Step 5: The bad experience is now just a speck in the distance at the far end of your timeline. As a consequence, you can no longer make out anything about it, nor hear anything.

Step 6: Run through the procedure again and again until the memory no longer bothers you.

The same timeline procedure can be used to retrieve positive memories, dust them off, and line them up, one after another, as a continuous and readily accessible sequence.

Step 1: Float back along your timeline looking for a pleasant memory.

Step 2: Lift out that memory, like removing one card from a card file.

[Handwritten at top: "nice ex to recall nice memories"]

Step 3: Now begin changing the qualities of the experience from those of a past event to those of an event that's just happened (see the previous exercise). At the same time, steadily bring the memory to the *near end* of your timeline right in front of your face.

Step 4: Enjoy the memory. Play it over and over, each time recovering more and more information.

Step 5: When you're satisfied, file the memory permanently in its new place, then float back along the timeline, select another memory and repeat the process.

Learning to see your past differently

The visualizations we've just completed are designed to help you forget the negative and remember the positive. But supposing there are things that bother you and yet you don't actually want to forget entirely? Maybe you think that you were weak, or unreasonable or inept? And that sort of negative self-evaluation lowers your self-esteem today. Nevertheless, you don't want to consign those chunks of experience to the end of your timeline because they have things to teach you and, anyway, they remain an important part of your life.

In NLP you can retain memories but see them very differently through a process known as reframing.

Jargon buster – reframing

Reframing is changing the meaning of something that's happened so you feel differently about it.

Consider the following situations and reframe them in a more positive way:
* Sue and Jasmine were giggling together in a corner – I'm sure they were having a joke at my expense.
* The boss came in this morning and didn't say a word to me – I think he's going to sack me.

2 transform your past

* My partner didn't want to make love last night – I think he/she isn't turned on by me any more.

In order to be happy, feel optimistic and behave positively, we need to reframe things in ways that are most advantageous to us. When people are giggling in a corner we can join in. When the boss isn't talking it could be that she or he has personal worries. When your partner isn't in the mood, the headache could be genuine.

The Decision Destroyer

The visualization that follows is something I've adapted from a standard NLP procedure known as the 'Decision Destroyer' (because it neutralizes poor decisions made in the past). You can use it whenever you can't see how an experience could be reframed in a more positive way.

Step 1: First, put yourself in the right state of mind. I'm going to suggest you search for feelings of capability, benevolence and humour – the way you might feel if a small child came to you with what seemed an overwhelming problem but which you could easily solve.

Step 2: Now intensify those feelings. You can do that by emphasizing the positive submodalities.

Step 3: Glide back over your timeline until you find a memory or sequence of memories you want to feel differently about. I emphasize that these are memories you want to keep but aspects of which nevertheless bother you – don't do this with memories you'd prefer to forget. Now look at yourself in this memory and – with those feelings of capability, benevolence and humour to the forefront – *absolve* yourself. Realize that you were younger and less experienced then. Remember the presupposition, 'There's no such thing as failure, only feedback.'

Step 4: Return to the present with the feedback and be grateful you can use that feedback in a positive way.

Step 5: Put the feedback to work for you, your partner, your relatives and your friends.

Dealing with anxieties, fears and phobias

When a phobia is caused by *a specific incident in your past* then NLP has a powerful method of dealing with it. It's called, very simply, the Fast Phobia Technique.

Think of something that makes you anxious. Then visualize it from *multiple perspectives*, moving from *first* to *second* to *third* position, and from *association* to *dissociation*.

Jargon buster – multiple perspectives

We usually visualize scenes from the past (or future) from our own perspective, but we can also take the perspective of other people involved or even of detached observers – **multiple perspectives**.

Jargon buster – first, second and third positions

- **First position** means visualizing something as seen through your own eyes.
- **Second position** means visualizing something through the eyes of any other person present.
- **Third position** means visualizing something through the eyes of an uninvolved outsider standing some distance away.

Some people are naturally very good at adopting multiple perspectives while others will need to make an effort. There are good reasons for acquiring this habit. One of them is the ability to *associate* with others and to *dissociate* from yourself.

> ### Jargon buster – association and dissociation
>
> - **Association** is to see, hear, touch, taste and smell everything from the perspective of a particular person and, above all, to respond emotionally as that person. Normally we associate with ourselves when we imagine things (first position), but it's also possible to associate with any other person in the scene (second position). This leads to empathy.
> - **Dissociation** is to stand back and not feel directly involved. We can dissociate from ourselves and everybody else by visualizing a scene through the eyes of someone completely uninvolved (third position). In that case, the emotional response will be far less.
> - Dissociation means stepping back and seeing yourself or the situation from outside. **Double-dissociation** means stepping even further back and watching yourself, as it were, watching yourself, so you feel even more removed and even safer emotionally.

[margin note: CINEMA EXERCISE]

The point of the above exercise is to get you used to the idea of changing perspectives. You should now have found that when you move to third position and dissociate, you don't feel things so strongly. In the Fast Phobia Technique that follows we're going to be revisiting the incident that caused your phobia in the first place. But you don't want to make yourself scared all over again, so we're not just going to dissociate, we're going to *double-dissociate*.

Step 1: Imagine that you're in a cinema. In this cinema you're going to be in as many as three places at once – appearing in the film, watching it as a customer and working as the projectionist, all at the same time. (That's the wonderful thing about the imagination – you can do anything you like.)

Step 2: Be a customer sitting in the cinema, watching a still black and white image of yourself on the screen the moment *before* you experienced this fear for the very first time. (If you

Fast Phobia

can't remember when you first had the fear, instead use an image of the moment before you experienced the fear the most intensely.)

Step 3: Now you're going to become the projectionist sitting in the projection booth. As the projectionist, you can now see yourself in the cinema as well as the image on screen.

Step 4: Still as the projectionist, you run the black and white movie of the frightening situation. You see everything but it means almost nothing to you because you're just the projectionist, sitting in the safety of your projection booth. When you get to the end of the movie, where the person in the film (you) is safe again, you stop the projector and freeze-frame.

Step 5: This is where things get really tricky. You have to leave the projection booth and step into the still picture on the screen. It now turns to full colour and as it does so, the movie runs backwards very quickly. In other words, everyone walks backwards and talks backwards. So it should all look and sound quite funny – and to underline how laughable it is you need to have a film score of comical music (the sort of thing you might hear at the circus). Hearing this music and the backwards voices and seeing the ridiculous movements, *laugh*.

Step 6: Repeat the backwards film sequence several more times, getting faster and faster each time.

If, after completing the six steps, the object of your fear still scores a three or higher on a scale of one to ten, repeat the procedure. If you rate it from zero to two, then go out in the real world and see what happens.

Increasing the impact of the fast phobia technique

Just because you have a phobia doesn't mean that you're necessarily very motivated to do anything about it. A lot of phobias are quite easy to live with. If you have a fear of heights, for example, or dogs, or swimming pools you can fairly easily keep away from them. Here's a way of goading yourself into performing the Fast Phobia Technique properly.

Think back to times you came face to face with your phobia *and were embarrassed by the way you behaved*. Try to think of five such occasions and then run them continuously in your mind, one after the other. Five encounters with spiders, five encounters with heights, five encounters with confined spaces, or whatever it might be. Then run those scenes again with everything magnified – make the pictures larger, the colours brighter and the sounds louder. And then run them a third time, very fast, with even greater magnification. Keep running that loop of five scenes until you really feel that the whole phobia thing has so ruined your life that you're desperate to put an end to it. That's the state of mind in which you should approach the Fast Phobia Technique.

Now let's look at the things you can do after employing the Fast Phobia Technique.

Richard Bandler has written in his book *Get The Life You Want* that after running the technique readers should get up from their chairs 'and test it, and test it, and test it' and that 'bit by bit' the phobia will disappear.

At the time of writing you can see him in action on YouTube in a two-part video called *The Hypnotist*. In this he treats a woman distressed by what she tells him is a phobia about flying brought on by a hijacking 27 years earlier. (In fact, Bandler diagnoses her not as suffering from a phobia but from panic attacks brought on by any enclosed environment and, indeed, that proves to be the case.)

Bandler augments the Fast Phobia Technique with spinning (see Chapter 1) and then takes her out for desensitization by gradual exposure. He has her ride in a lift with other people, a situation she normally finds overwhelming. From there he takes her to a cinema. (This also has the effect of piling on the pressure and increasing her motivation, as described above.) The final test is to take a flight. During this the patient again suffers a panic attack but overcomes it.

So it was a success for NLP but not an instant success and, realistically, you shouldn't expect to do better on yourself than Richard Bandler did.

A final tip. Whenever you're desensitizing yourself through gradual exposure it helps enormously to have a laugh. Take some friends with you, having first primed them to kid around, tell jokes, tickle you and generally divert your conscious attention from your fears.

3

transform your learning abilities

Education is *everything*. Yes, it can sound rather boring. A stage of your life you thought you'd left behind along with school uniforms and tedious rules.

But there is another way of looking at it. Supposing you had the ability to do anything and everything you ever wanted? Wouldn't life be incredible? Every day would be a great adventure. Each morning you'd wake up and ask yourself what new skill you were going to master next. Acting? Ballroom dancing? Calligraphy? Drawing? A foreign language? Geology? Horse riding? A musical instrument? Sailing? Share trading? Tantric sex? Zen? How endlessly fascinating life would be! How fascinating *you* would be! Well, it can be that way. And you already know the NLP presupposition:

Anything anyone else can do, you can do.

Broadly speaking there are two stages to the modelling process, implicit and explicit.

> ### Jargon buster – implicit and explicit modelling
>
> **Implicit modelling** means unconsciously *absorbing* what someone else does, without asking questions and without applying verbal descriptions.
>
> **Explicit modelling** means consciously deducing which of the expert's actions you've now absorbed are important and which are irrelevant.

Modelling is the way infants acquire knowledge and skills. They observe – the implicit phase. Then they try things out for themselves. What works they keep, what doesn't work they reject – the explicit phase.

Step 1: Find your model. Ideally, this is the world's greatest expert. Your model also has to be someone you can observe in depth for a sufficient period of time. That's easy in some disciplines, much harder in others.

Step 2: Prepare for each modelling session by getting yourself in a heightened state of awareness. You could try the Betty Erickson self-hypnosis method described in Chapter 1 – when required to state the purpose you say something like: 'I am entering into a state of self-hypnosis so that I can hand over to my unconscious mind the task of absorbing the techniques used by my model.'

Step 3: Observe your model in action. Do *not* make any attempt to describe what's going on, either by writing it down, or describing it out loud, or even by thinking it in words. Nor should you ask any questions. Simply try to absorb.

Step 4: As soon as you feel able, try copying your model. Continue observing and copying until you can do the same things.

The explicit modelling phase

At the end of the implicit phase you can reproduce the same results as your chosen expert. That, anyway, would be the case in an ideal modelling situation. But you still don't necessarily know *how* you're doing it. In the explicit modelling phase you therefore use 'subtraction'. That's to say, you leave something out and see what happens.

Let's say you had been modelling Milton Erickson and you had noticed that at a certain point he began breathing very audibly and very slowly. Is that something that contributed to the hypnotic effect? Having precisely copied everything Milton Erickson did, and having obtained the same results that he obtained, you would, on another occasion, omit the slow, audible breathing and see what happened. If you still got the original result you would know the breathing was superfluous. Conversely, if your technique was no longer successful, you would know the breathing was crucial.

Clearly, the explicit phase can be laborious and time-consuming. There could be hundreds of things to check. You may well conclude that, for your purposes, it's enough to be able to get the results you want, even if some of the things you're doing are irrelevant. On the other hand, if you want to be a world-beater that's the kind of attention to detail that's essential.

Here are some suggestions:
* If you can model exceptional people, so much the better.
* The easiest way of pinning an expert down is usually to pay for lessons. Choose someone who understands implicit modelling and is amenable to you following that approach. Another possibility would be to get a job working for the model.
* Don't just watch your model from first position — also try to become the person you're modelling, seeing what they're seeing and feeling what they're feeling from second position.

* You can effectively extend the observation period by making your own videos and playing them back again and again... and again. Professionally made DVDs will probably never show all the things you need, unless the film makers are experienced modellers, but in the absence of a flesh-and-blood expert they're better than nothing and, like your own videos, you can watch them over and over. You may also find clips of useful models on websites such as YouTube. As well as watching at normal speed, use slow motion and freeze-frame.
* You may think you're faithfully copying your expert, but can you be sure? Have someone film you.
* Some people dress like their models, take on their mannerisms and habits, and learn to speak like them. It might sound extreme, even a little crazy, but it can be effective.

Belief

In order to be able to do something you have to believe you can do it.

Here's a visualization to remind you how enormous your learning ability truly is.

Step 1: Close your eyes, travel back in time and imagine yourself as an infant. See yourself crawling about on the floor. Think of how enormous everything seems, how impossibly huge. Really enter into the experience. Look up at the table towering above you. Take hold of the leg and haul yourself up. You're standing upright for the very first time in your life. You did it! And now everything else looks just that little bit more manageable.

Step 2: Think of the sound of voices as you lie in your cot. They're no more meaningful than the noises made by people speaking, say, Russian or Chinese today. You can't even tell where one noise ends and another noise begins. But you're persistent. Day after day you listen and gradually you learn to recognize patterns and isolate one noise from another. Day after day you try to copy the sounds. And one day you say, 'Dada'. You've just spoken your very first word.

Step 3: See yourself at school. You're very tiny. Your feet don't even touch the floor as you sit at the table. A book is open in front of you. There's a big colour picture and underneath it some black marks. You put your finger by the black marks and, slowly and laboriously, you spell out 'd... o... g'. You've just read your very first word.

Step 4: Now think about whatever it is you wish to learn today. How difficult can it be compared with all that you already achieved as an infant? Not very difficult at all.

How we learned as a child

Good Ex for helping overcome new learning challenges

3 transform your learning abilities

4

transform your inner voice

What are you doing today that makes you feel nervous? Maybe you're going to the bank to ask for a loan. Maybe you have a job interview. Maybe it's a horse riding lesson. And it doesn't help that someone is telling you, 'You're not going to be able to pull this off.' *Who* on earth would say a thing like that? In fact, it's the same person who for years has been telling you you're not attractive, not witty, not smart, and generally not much good at anything. And that person is ... *you*.

We all have an inner voice. Or even several different ones. The problem is that most people's inner voices are unrelentingly negative. They tend to say things like, 'What's the matter with you? You really made a mess of that... *again*. Can't you do anything right?' And so on.

If you have a negative inner voice, then it's in for a little bit of a shock. Richard Bandler recounts that he often tells his to 'Shut the f*** up!'

If yours is saying anything negative, do the same — right now. It helps, sometimes quite a lot. But NLP also has a few rather more sophisticated techniques.

Discrediting an inner voice

Rather than simply trying to shout louder than your inner voice, a more effective method is to *discredit* it. Inner voices are convincing but they aren't necessarily any more right than any other voices.

One way *not* to believe it is to *change* the voice. Right now it probably sounds authoritative. But what if it were to sound like the voice of the politician you most distrust? Then maybe you wouldn't take such notice of it.

Step 1: Think of a person you greatly distrust. It could be someone you know, it could be a contemporary politician or it could be a historical figure such as Hitler. Hear their voice and identify what qualities (submodalities) in the voice make you distrustful. Is there something about the pitch, perhaps? The rhythm? The timbre?

Step 2: Now think of the negative thing your inner voice has been telling you, but instead of hearing the usual voice, hear instead the distrusted voice, complete with all those unreliable, cheating, lying submodalities.

Step 3: Now push that distrusted voice and its distrusted, negative message further and further away from you until it gets fainter and fainter and you can't hear it any more.

40   kickstart your life with NLP

Step 4: Check to see how you now feel – hopefully a lot less negative.

Step 5: Future pace (see below) by visualizing yourself successfully doing the very thing your negative voice had been telling you that you couldn't do.

Step 6: Actually *do* the thing your negative voice had been telling you that you couldn't do.

Jargon buster – future pacing

Future pacing simply means visualizing a scene in the future in which you behave in the way you want. That will help you install the new behaviour in your unconscious.

Swish your doubts away

Sometimes it's more a case of being overwhelmed by a general *feeling* of doubt than by specific criticisms. A special visualization known as the Swish can help.

Jargon buster – Swishing

Swishing means swapping one mental image for another so quickly that the submodalities from the first image become transposed to the second. It can be used in all kinds of ways. Always remember to carry out an ecology check (see Chapter 1) before Swishing or trying to change your unconscious by any method.

Step 1: Think of some quality or ability in yourself about which you have doubts that you'd like to sweep away. Now identify the submodalities that are associated with doubt. Do you, perhaps, get a fluttering feeling in your stomach? Is the visualization blurry? Is the image in a particular position?

Step 2: Clear that visualization away by saying your telephone number backwards.

Step 3: Now think of some positive quality in yourself about which you have no doubts at all, about which you feel only certainty. How about your love for your children? Or your dog? Or your home town? Call up an image that exemplifies that certainty (Image 2). Now identify the submodalities associated with certainty. Perhaps you feel something rising up in your chest that makes you want to punch the air? Is the visualization clear? Is it, perhaps, very colourful?

Step 4: Fully experience certainty and the image associated with certainty (Image 2) and then, suddenly, Swish (that's to say, swap) that image, and only the image, for the image about which you have doubts (Image 1). It's essential that you maintain the submodalities associated with certainty – and all the feelings associated with certainty – and that you attach them to Image 1, so you see yourself succeeding.

Step 5: You should now begin to feel about Image 1 the same way you felt about Image 2. That's to say, certainty about your ability to succeed. Repeat the process several times straight off. Then go out and test the result by doing the very thing about which you previously doubted yourself.

Step 6: Continue to alternate the visualization exercise and the practical test until your doubts are gone.

Reframing the negative

Step 1: Think of a situation about which your inner voice has been saying negative things. It could be something from the past or it could be something you're going to be doing in the future.

Step 2: Freeze-frame the single moment from your internal movie that most encapsulates that negativity.

Step 3: Now try playing around with the image. If there are people who intimidate you, why not cut them down to size? Literally – make them little. Why not give them some accessories? Maybe funny hats and red noses. How do you see yourself? Why not portray yourself like a hero or an Amazon from a classical painting? When you're satisfied with the revised image, experiment with different colours, textures, backgrounds and so on. For example, you could make it into a cartoon, a photo-realistic oil painting or maybe a moody watercolour. Once you've discovered the style that most helps you to feel the way you'd like to feel, fix it in your mind.

Using multiple perspectives

Changing perspectives is a useful technique whenever your negative inner voice is really laying it on thick. And especially when it's providing frightening images to discourage you. 'Look at this,' it says. 'This is how you're going to look after you've crashed/fallen over/made an idiot of yourself in front of all those people.'

We first encountered multiple perspectives in Chapter 2. The one we want here is third position or dissociation. In other words, we're going to minimize the emotional impact by adopting the position of an outsider.

For example, let's say that you're at the top of a steep ski slope – a black run. You want to do it but you're apprehensive. From the bottom it hadn't looked so bad but now you're up here it looks horribly dangerous. The answer in this case is to switch to the perspective of someone at the bottom of the run looking up and seeing you. In other words, you dissociate from your predicament. Now it doesn't seem so steep, does it? Watch yourself coming down – and make it good.

Narrow camera angle

Narrow camera angle is a variation on multiple perspectives that I use quite a lot in intimidating physical situations. It's basically an elaboration of the traditional advice given to people scared of heights: 'Don't look down'. You remain associated (that's to say, in first position) but you limit your field of view, both via your eyes *and in your imagination* to things that are familiar and harmless. It also works with things like visits to the dentist.

Questioning an inner voice

So far we've learned to shut out, ignore and overwrite negativity and doubt. What we're going to do next is analyse what the negative inner voice is saying and uncover the holes in its arguments.

According to Bandler and Grinder, much of the success achieved by the therapists Fritz Perls and Virginia Satir was due to this very process of confronting their clients' inner voices.

In effect, Perls and Satir would bring about change simply by asking questions whenever they encountered damaging examples of generalization, deletion or distortion. For example, if a client said 'everyone' was against them the question might be, 'Everyone?' In that deceptively simple way, the client would be forced to acknowledge the generalization and look at things differently.

Turning your inner voice into a constructive partner

Once you've successfully challenged a negative inner voice, the next step is to get a constructive dialogue going.

A good starting point is the NLP presupposition:

Underlying every behaviour is a positive intention.

In other words, when your inner voice tells you you're useless, it's doing it for a good reason. You need to find out that reason. How? Simply by starting a conversation, like this:

You: 'Why do you keep criticizing me?'

Inner voice: 'Because I want you to sharpen up and pay attention to what you're doing.'

You: 'Well, you're having completely the opposite effect because you're demoralizing me.'

Inner voice: 'So you're weak on top of everything else! Can't take criticism!'

You: 'I'm telling you, if you don't improve I'm getting rid of you.'

Inner voice: 'You wish! Listen, you've got to stop making stupid mistakes.'

You: 'So tell me how. Be more constructive.'

Inner voice: 'All right. You need more patience. Be willing to spend a little more time on preparation before you rush into things. Then you'll be fine.'

You: 'Why couldn't you have put it like that to begin with?'

Did you find that conversation comical or even absurd? If so, you're going to find Six Step Reframing something of a revelation, because you'll be talking to your unconscious in just this way as if it's a separate person. Developed by John Grinder, it's a technique that can be used to change all kinds of behaviour. In this example, we're using it to change the negativity of your unconscious as regards, let's say, any potentially dangerous physical activity. At first Six Step Reframing may well strike you as a little wacky. However, once you try it you'll fairly soon get used to the idea.

Step 1: Identify the behaviour to be changed – in this example, it's the negativity of your unconscious.

Step 2: Get your unconscious to communicate via a reliable involuntary signal. Grinder suggests asking something like: 'Will you, my unconscious, communicate with me?' You must then wait passively with your attention focused on your body for a signal from your unconscious. If you receive a signal, touch the area of your body where the signal occurred and say 'Thank you'. To check, you then ask: 'If the signal just offered means "Yes", please repeat it.' You now need to validate the signal. Asking your unconscious to remain inactive, you now try to reproduce the signal consciously. If you can, then the possibility exists that the signal wasn't a genuine signal from the unconscious and you'll need to repeat the process until you have an authentic involuntary signal.

Step 3: Discover the positive intention behind the behaviour to be changed. In this case you could ask your unconscious: 'What is the positive intention behind the negative comments?' Let's assume you get the answer, 'To prevent you doing something in which you might get hurt.'

Step 4: Having discovered the positive intention, you now need to generate a set of alternatives as good as or better than the original behaviour at satisfying that positive intention. Ask your unconscious: 'Develop an alternative range of behaviours – all of which satisfy the positive intention while nevertheless helping me achieve my goal – and from those select up to three for implementation. When you have completed the task, give me a positive signal.'

Step 5: The alternative behaviours should now be apparent to you. For example, your unconscious might agree to drop the negative comments if you a) accept the need to take more lessons, b) agree to practise the basic manoeuvres more thoroughly, c) be willing to wear protective clothing. Get your unconscious to accept responsibility for implementing the new behaviours. For example, you might ask: 'Will you, my unconscious mind, take responsibility for making sure the new behaviours are followed?'

Step 6: Carry out an ecology check (see Chapter 1) by asking your unconscious to make sure that none of the new behaviours will cause a problem for you or for others.

Obviously some kinds of negative thoughts are essential, otherwise we'd very soon do things that resulted in injury and even death. What we're concerned with here are thoughts that unnecessarily undermine our abilities and restrain our progress. *I'd never be able to do that. That's too hard for me. I'll never be any good.* And so on. As an experiment, try making a record every time you have an incorrect negative thought during the course of a single day. The easiest way is to mark a dot in a notebook or on the back of your hand. You'll probably be astonished by how many dots you accumulate by bedtime. That's why it's so effective to transform your inner voice into one that's working positively for your advancement.

5
transform your success

As Richard Bandler likes to point out, if you're looking for difficulties you'll always find them. Instead, he says, you should be looking to see what *works*. In the last chapter we learned how *not* to look for difficulties. In this chapter we're going to examine the second part of his prescription and learn how to increase optimism, confidence and positivity.

Let's start right at the beginning of the day. What time is that for you? Maybe an austere 6 a.m.? A more relaxed 7.30 a.m.? Or perhaps a thoroughly decadent 9 a.m.? In fact, the day doesn't start when you wake up. A day starts *when you go to bed*. It's what you do *then* that sets the tone for the next 24 hours.

So what you do is not only prime yourself to wake up *before* the alarm, but wake up full of optimism. Bandler says he wants people to wake up and ask: 'How much fun can I have today?'; 'How much freedom can I find?'; 'How much more can I do than I've ever done before?' Programming that attitude is done the night before.

All you have to do, when you're drifting off, is say something along these lines: 'I am now going to have a wonderful night's sleep, and when I wake up at 7 a.m. I will feel completely refreshed and full of enthusiasm and optimism for the things I am going to be doing.'

Elaborate on that as you wish.

Getting motivated

Okay. So you're up. You're feeling good. Now you need to motivate yourself for the next big step.

NLP makes a distinction between two different kinds of motivation:

* motivation *away* from something
* motivation *towards* something.

You can be motivated *away* from discomfort, confrontation, criticism, fear, pain, embarrassment, failure and so on, just as you can be motivated *towards* comfort, tranquillity, praise, success and much more.

Nobody is wholly 'away from' or 'towards' but – for any given type of situation – we all have a tendency to be mostly one or the other. In order to motivate yourself effectively, it helps to understand your own personality in this respect.

Stoking up motivation

Having decided what kind of motivation works best with you, you can then stoke it up.

Suppose that, for various reasons, you wish to give up something – for example, gambling. You've tried and you've failed. And the reason is this. You're motivated to stop gambling but your motivation to continue gambling is even stronger. Let's suppose you're an 'away from' person. What you have to do is stoke up your motivation *not* to gamble, until it overwhelms your motivation *to* gamble. In other words, to get you to the point at which you say 'enough is enough'. This is how to bring on that feeling through visualization.

Step 1: Think of five negative scenes connected with gambling (or whatever it might be). You could, for example, visualize the arrival of household bills you can't pay because you've lost money. You might think of how upset your partner is. You might think of the toll the stress is taking on your health. And so on.

Step 2: Run the five scenes in your mind one after the other to make your own 'anti-gambling' film. Then run them all again but faster. Then again, faster still. Continue until you have the overwhelming feeling 'enough is enough'.

The Circle of Confidence

The Circle of Confidence is a technique for transferring confidence from a situation in which you feel mastery to a situation in which you feel inadequate. Some people climb mountains or sail round the world single-handed to try to convince themselves that they can have the self-confidence to tackle just about any situation. They theorize that if they take on the world's hardest challenges, then nothing else will ever seem difficult again. But life isn't quite like that.

NLP does things differently. It allows you to take the self-confidence you felt in any previous situation, including one that was *easy*, and then it transfers that feeling to the more difficult situation.

This is my variation on the Circle of Confidence, which I've found works well.

Step 1: Something important is coming up. Think of a quality you'll need if you're going to handle that situation to the best of your abilities. In this example we're focusing on confidence, but you could also use the procedure for other qualities.

Step 2: Search your memory for a past situation in which you felt that necessary confidence. It doesn't have to have been an especially difficult situation. Relive that confident time, seeing and hearing everything in as much detail as possible. Particularly notice how you looked and how the confidence was oozing out of you.

Step 3: Imagine a circle on the floor. Take the confidence you feel and pour it into the circle. Immediately the circle takes on a colour – the colour that, to you, is the colour of confidence. It also makes a noise. Maybe it's a buzzing sound or even music – again, it's whatever expresses confidence to you.

Step 4: Are there any other qualities you'll need? Maybe patience? Maybe judgement? If so, repeat the procedure, also pouring those qualities into your circle.

Step 5: Turn your thoughts to the future occasion when you'll want to feel those qualities. Select a cue to that moment. For example, if you're going to give a speech, the cue could be someone introducing you. Or, if you're going to an interview, it could be a secretary calling your name. (But don't make it too specific otherwise you might never get the cue you envisaged.)

Step 6: Holding that cue in your mind, step into the circle and visualize all those qualities rising up from the floor, permeating and enveloping you. As you move around, that cocoon of confidence will move with you.

Step 7: Visualize the future unfolding from that cue moment. See yourself behaving with confidence and all the other qualities you've selected.

good for coaching someone

Step 8: When the cue moment arrives for real, visualize the circle on the floor, step into it and go and do what you have to do.

Swishing confidence

Step 1: Your first task is to think of the kind of situation in which you have felt inadequate in the past. Really enter into that unsatisfactory experience. See, hear, smell, taste and touch as much of it as possible. This is the cue image.

Step 2: Clear the screen. If you find it difficult to clear your head, try reciting your telephone number backwards.

Step 3: Now you're going to build an image of yourself the way you'd *like* to be. The way you'd look and feel if you had complete mastery of the cue image situation and *had already successfully dealt with it*. We'll call this version 'wonderful you'. Spend plenty of time building the image of 'wonderful you'. Finally, give 'wonderful you' something to say that really encapsulates how you'd like to feel after having triumphed. It could be, 'I'm the master of this situation' or 'I never fail' or 'Easy!' or whatever you want.

Step 4: Take the image of 'wonderful you' and compress it into a sparkling dot. Place the dot into a blank screen and then let it grow and grow until it fills the screen. Hear 'wonderful you' speaking the words you decided in Step 3. Repeat this step over and over until you can reliably conjure up the sparkling dot and expand it.

Step 5: Place the sparkling dot into the centre of the cue image from Step 1 and Swish. Make that bothersome cue image fade and disintegrate while the sparkling dot gets bigger and brighter and clearer. If you already know what success would look like, then visualize 'wonderful you' behaving in that way in the expanded dot. For example, if you were nervous about a snowboarding manoeuvre, you could visualize 'wonderful you' perfectly emulating what you've seen experts do. On the other hand, if you don't know the solution then just visualize 'wonderful you' speaking the words from Step 3.

Step 6: Create a break by having a completely blank screen appear.

Step 7: Repeat Steps 4 to 6, getting faster and faster. It's impossible to say how many times will be necessary. Some people find two or three times are enough, others need ten and still others twenty.

The New Behaviour Generator

So now you're up, you're motivated and you're confident. But how would you like that confidence to manifest itself? How precisely do you want to behave? What do you actually want to *do*?

You can use the New Behaviour Generator to translate that feeling of confidence into a whole scenario.

Step 1: Identify the new behaviour you would like to have. For this example, let's say you want to be more expansive and charismatic.

Step 2: You are the director of a movie in which you are also the star. As the director, give instructions to yourself about the way you should behave. Watch yourself exhibit the new behaviour. In your role as director, make any corrections or changes you think necessary.

Step 3: Once you're satisfied, step into the movie and experience what it's like to have this new way of behaving, as seen through your own eyes as the star. Not only see but, of course, hear everything and feel what it's like. (In other words, you've now switched from third position to first position, from dissociation to association.) Note the reaction of other people. Is it what you want it to be? Also check that this new behaviour really is suitable for you.

Step 4: If you're not happy with anything, return to your role as director, make the necessary changes and repeat Step 3.

Step 5: Use future pacing. Visualize a situation in the future where you will want to behave in this new way. Look for a cue that could be used to trigger the behaviour automatically. For example, it might be the door to your boss's office, your partner shouting or your children squabbling. Imagine yourself seeing or hearing the cue and immediately adopting the new behaviour. Play this 'film' as often as necessary until the new behaviour feels natural.

Step 6: Use the new behaviour in a real situation.

How to anchor a behaviour

Wouldn't it be useful if you could actually program yourself so the desired response was *automatic*? So that no matter what self-doubts or negative emotions you had, you nevertheless could accomplish the task, and perform it to a high standard. Well you can certainly help yourself by using the technique of 'anchoring'.

Jargon buster – anchoring

In their book *Trance-formations*, Bandler and Grinder say that '**anchoring** refers to the tendency for any one element of an experience to bring back the entire experience'. NLP uses that perfectly natural phenomenon to create artificial triggers.

If you're driving a car and you see brake lights go on ahead of you, without even thinking, you take your foot off the accelerator and move it to the brake pedal. In this example, brake lights are the trigger (or anchor) and the action of braking is the programmed response. (Notice, however, that the anchor doesn't actually *compel* you to brake – you retain your freedom to perform a different action if you judge that the situation demands it.)

Skilled hypnotists can use quite unrelated stimuli as anchors, but when you're using this technique on yourself it will work better if the anchor is as natural and logical as possible.

In the example that follows, we'll be anchoring a feeling of patience. But you can adapt this procedure for anything you want.

Step 1: Choose your anchors. For patience, I'm going to suggest you stroke your chin, which involves the optimum three senses. It is:

* a visual anchor – the sight of your hand coming up to your chin and moving in front of your chin
* an audible anchor – the sound of your fingers against the skin of your face; behind the concealment of your hand you could also whisper the word 'patience'
* a kinaesthetic anchor – the feeling of your fingers against the skin of your face.

Step 2: Think of a time when you felt truly serene, calm, imperturbable and – above all – patient. Remember the NLP presupposition that we already have within us all the resources we need. However, if you really can't recall such a time, then imagine the feeling or recall a film in which someone you admire exhibited supreme patience.

Step 3: Revel in that feeling of patience. See, hear, touch, taste and smell everything to do with that patience. Spin it up as described in Chapter 1.

Step 4: Just *before* your feeling of patience reaches its peak, set your anchors by gently stroking your chin and whispering the word 'patience'. Repeat the process several times.

Step 5: Future pace by visualizing a scene that demands patience and watch yourself responding with patience.

Step 6: As soon as possible, deliberately seek out a situation that will test your patience a little. Fire your anchors. Over the next few days, keep on experiencing irritating situations and keep on firing your anchors. You will need to deal successfully with maybe a score of situations before the anchor will become permanent and automatic.

The more you use an anchor, the more powerful it becomes. We're all familiar with the way sportsmen punch the air or do a little dance when they've scored. What they're doing is 'stacking' an anchor. Each time they perform that ritual they add the power of that new victory to all their previous victories. That, in turn, creates the psychological impression of an unstoppable momentum of success.

Rewriting your future

Step 1: Picture the scene of your future success in as much detail as possible, noticing the colours, the sounds, the smells and so on.

Step 2: Put yourself into that scene and see yourself achieving your goal. Watch and listen as if you were at the cinema.

Step 3: In your role as director, improve the impact of the 'film' in every way you can. Perhaps you can use more close-ups. Different camera angles. Slow motion. Freeze-frames. Music for emphasis. A voice-over saying what a great thing you've achieved. Really revel in the whole thing. See it. Hear it. Touch it. Taste it. Smell it. It's real.

Step 4: Look backwards from the scene of your triumph to where you are today. See the road that brought you to your goal.

Step 5: Slowly amble back along the side of the road and identify the various steps that brought you to your goal. Don't rush. There could have been all kinds of factors and you need to identify every one. Ask yourself what personal qualities you brought to bear to reach your goal. What actions did you take? What other people were involved? How did you relate to them? As you go, write down all the steps in sequence.

Step 6: Once back in the present, consult your list and begin putting it into action.

6
transform your health

NLP is hardly alone in taking the view that the mind and the body form one system. Let's call it the 'bodymind'. Our bodies affect the way we think, and the way we think affects our bodies. Since NLP is all about the way we think, especially at the unconscious level, it should also be very good at improving our health in all kinds of ways.

Richard Bandler recounts how, when he had a stroke, a doctor in the emergency ward told him: 'No matter what anyone says to you, no matter who they are, I am telling you, you can make a full recovery.'

A few days later another doctor told Bandler he would be paralysed for the rest of his life. But Bandler chose, instead, to think of what he had been told in the emergency ward: 'I would focus every fibre in my soul,' he wrote, 'in being able to first move my toes and then my feet and then my knees...'.

He didn't think about what he *couldn't* do. That would have created a sense of failure. Instead, he focused on what he was succeeding at. Moving just one toe was a success and became the platform for moving two toes. And so on.

Step 1: Deal with any negative prognostications by giving the speakers voices you don't trust. Once you've got rid of that negativity, never think about those prognostications again.

Step 2: Promise yourself you *will* make a full recovery. Think of all the difficult situations you've come through in the past. Take this determination and spin it up (as described in Chapter 1).

Step 3: Visualize yourself getting better and better.

Step 4: Visualize a time in the future when you *are* fully recovered. Revel in that experience. See, feel, hear, taste and smell what it's like to be fully recovered. Adjust the submodalities to make the experience of being fully recovered as vivid as possible.

Step 5: Repeat Steps 2–4 several times a day until you *are* better.

When you have more minor ailments, a simple visualization when you're going off to sleep at night can help. Bedtime is a good moment for this because it gives you good access to your unconscious just when your bodymind is best able to repair itself. For example, let's say that you've damaged your Achilles tendon.

Step 1: Get yourself nicely relaxed in bed and begin drifting off to sleep.

Step 2: Focus on an image of health and identify the submodalities. Is the sun shining, for example? Is your skin shining? Is there a particular feeling in your body? Do you hear anything?

Step 3: Set a target for the bodymind to aim at, by visualizing yourself as completely healthy. Turn up all the submodalities associated with health. See that the part or parts of your body associated with your current problem (in this case your Achilles tendon) are entirely sound and well.

Step 4: Visualize yourself saying something along the following lines: 'I am well. My Achilles tendon (or whatever part of the body is affected) is completely healthy.' You can go on to describe how wonderful it is, how strong, elastic and controlled (or whatever).

Step 5: Continue like this until you fall asleep.

Giving up isn't so hard to do

Being healthy means doing certain things. It also means not doing other things, such as smoking, overeating or drinking large quantities of alcohol.

Here's how you can motivate yourself *not* to do something.

Have a go

Step 1: Think of five occasions on which your habit or addiction made you frightened for your health or disgusted with your behaviour. If alcohol is the problem, for example, then you might recall wasting large sums of money, saying hurtful things you later regretted, vomiting, having a terrible hangover, and being unable to do your job properly. If the problem is smoking, you could visualize the smoke funnelling into your lungs and leaving behind a fine layer of carcinogenic dust, having teeth removed because smoking has caused gum disease, being rebuffed by someone you were attracted to because they found your breath too disgusting, and so on. Experience those images to the full. Really see, feel, hear, taste and smell everything.

Step 2: Make a movie of your habit or addiction by running the five scenes in your mind, one after the other.

Step 3: Keep running them faster and faster until you really feel you want to end this behaviour for ever.

Modelling for health

If you find it hard to believe that life can be worth living without large quantities of alcohol, or chocolate, or fat, or if you find it hard to believe that exercise can be fun, then it might be worthwhile modelling someone who has a healthy lifestyle. If you grew up in an unhealthy household then being unhealthy may seem normal to you. You need to replace that concept with a new model.

Do you know anybody who has an especially healthy lifestyle? It needs to be someone you admire, otherwise you'll only confirm your own prejudices against healthy living (for example, that healthy people are boring).

As usual with modelling, just try to absorb their way of being without asking too many questions initially. Here are some of the things you might pay attention to:

* how many hours they sleep
* how much exercise they take
* how many portions of fruit and vegetables they eat
* how much alcohol they drink
* how often they get stressed and angry.

In this instance, the point of modelling is not for you to pioneer new ways of achieving optimum health (thousands of researchers are already engaged in that) but for you to be able to experience the fact that there are people who can be healthy *and happy*.

Dealing with stress

Stress can be both good and bad for your health.

In Chapter 5 you learned how to Swish for confidence. When you feel confident, you automatically feel less stress — so that's a useful tool. In Chapter 5 you also learned about anchoring. If you've forgotten how to do it, turn back and re-read that section because we're now going to add to your repertoire with a way of anchoring relaxation.

Step 1: Recall a time when you felt *incredibly* relaxed. Fully experience that sense of relaxation. Feel, see, hear, smell and taste the elements that made you that way. Identify the submodalities for relaxation.

Step 2: Create a break state by saying your telephone number backwards.

Step 3: Select three different kinds of anchors. A convenient kinaesthetic anchor might be stroking the sides of your face between your thumb and forefinger. An auditory anchor could simply be whispering the word 'relax' to yourself or recalling a tranquil piece of music (or both together). A visual anchor might be recalling the scene from Step 1.

Step 4: Re-experience the relaxation you created in Step 1. Take the submodalities for relaxation and adjust them until you're approaching the optimum level but not quite there. At that very moment, fire your three anchors.

Step 5: Create a break state by saying your telephone number backwards.

Step 6: Repeat Step 4 several times. On each occasion, try to improve the whole thing so that you feel more and more relaxed and your anchor-setting technique gets better and better.

Step 7: Fire your anchors. If you feel relaxed as a result then the procedure has worked.

Step 8: Future pace. Think of future potentially distressing situations in which you would like to feel more at ease. As you do so, fire your anchors. This will set things up for you so that when those situations come about you'll already be primed to become relaxed.

Step 9: Live life and whenever you encounter stressful situations for real, fire your anchors. The more often you repeat the procedure and the more often you use the anchors the more powerful the effect will be.

7

transform your powers of persuasion

The Milton Model is a powerful technique for influencing people – not in the usual way by asking direct questions and giving direct orders, but by behaving almost in the opposite manner, telling stories, and saying things that are vague and ambiguous. How ethical it is to use these techniques is something for you to decide, according to the circumstances.

Of course, Erickson used them to help people overcome problems, for which they had willingly come to consult him. In the cut and thrust of the business world you might also see them as legitimate. But at home, with people you love and who trust you, it would depend very much on your intentions. It has to be said that these techniques cannot force anyone to do anything; they just add to your persuasive powers.

Hypnotherapists have to be very aware of the effect they're having. They have to know when someone is genuinely in a trance or merely pretending to be in trance. They have to know when someone's going deeper and when they're coming out. They have to know when someone is visualizing something. They have to know when the visualization is pleasurable and when it's painful. They have to know when the words they're saying are working and when they're creating resistance.

This ability to calibrate is known in NLP as 'sensory acuity'. Here are some fun exercises to develop your own sensory acuity. Obviously you're going to be looking out for facial expression but also more subtle signals, such as eye movements, posture, breathing and muscle tone.

Have a go

Step 1: Ask a friend some simple questions that require only 'Yes' or 'No' answers.

Step 2: Note the body language that goes with 'Yes' and the body language that goes with 'No'.

Step 3: Now pose further questions, asking your friend not to reply out loud but simply to *think* 'Yes' or 'No'. From your observations of their body language you should be able to say accurately what the correct answers are.

This is one of the easiest calibrating exercises because most people will give, at least, a slight nod for a 'Yes' and a slight shake for a 'No'. Other signs might be tipping the head forward for a 'Yes' and back for a 'No', or warmer eyes for a 'Yes' and colder eyes for a 'No'.

Have a go

Step 1: When you're next talking with someone, say something inoffensive about them you know is *not* true. Calibrate.

Step 2: Follow up with something inoffensive you know *is* true. Calibrate.

Step 3: Repeat this a few times until you've identified all the body language that goes with incorrect and correct statements.

For example, you might say: 'If I remember correctly your partner works for an oil company' or 'Didn't you once live in South America?'

Have a go

Step 1: Ask a friend to think of someone he or she likes. Calibrate.

Step 2: Ask the friend to think of someone he or she hates. Calibrate.

Step 3: Repeat until you've identified all the body language.

Step 4: When you've got that clear, tell your friend that you're going to ask various questions about these two people but that you *don't* want your friend to tell you the answers. Instead, *you* will tell your friend the answers. All your friend has to do is look at you and nod when the answer is ready.

Step 5: Ask your friend questions, that require comparisons to be made between the person liked and the person hated. For example, you could ask: 'Which one has the largest feet?', 'Which one has the most freckles?' or 'Which one has the largest nose?' This works best if you ask questions that require your friend to conjure up images before answering. (A question such as 'Which one is tallest?' may be answered without much thought if the height difference is significant, and therefore without much change in body language.)

Step 6: After putting each question, observe your friend closely. He or she will think of one person then the other as the comparison is made. The answer will be the person your friend is thinking of just before looking at you and nodding – and you'll know which one that is by calibrating.

The signals to watch for ... and give

How did you get on with the calibration exercises? You should have learned a great deal about body language. Here are some of the things you should be taking note of and learning to match and mirror when appropriate.

Voice

We all instinctively tend to modify our language to be more like that of the people we're with.

As an exercise, first of all try matching fairly closely then switch to a different pattern – faster/slower, louder/softer – and see if the other person begins to follow you.

NLP makes a great deal about primary representational systems, and the subject is certainly worth knowing about. NLP holds that when people process information they tend to favour one of three methods, and that's reflected in the way they speak:

* they see visual images
* they hear sounds
* they experience feelings.

If you notice that someone leans heavily towards one system or another then it's worth following suit to tune in and establish rapport.

Posture and mannerisms

In fact, most human communication is non-verbal. Probably about 80 per cent. That might surprise you. But just think about it for a moment. What are your feelings about men with shaven heads? Or long hair? Or earrings? Or men or women with tattoos? Wearing kaftans? Green wellies? Chewing gum?

These are all things that are liable to cause some reaction in you. You have been communicated with. Whether or not you accurately decode the communication is another matter – but communication it is. And to establish rapport, all you have to do is copy.

Don't be in any way obvious, of course. If the other person even suspects anything, they'll think you're weird or making fun of them. The matching and mirroring has to be extremely subtle, just as it is when it's natural. The difference is that you're doing it on purpose, either to accelerate rapport or to create rapport with someone you normally wouldn't get on with.

You can also deliberately break rapport, perhaps to bring a conversation to an end. Sucking air in through the teeth and raising the shoulders, as if to stand up, is a standard signal. Looking away and giving a shrug is another. Or you might abruptly change the tempo to a rapid 'winding-up' speed.

Eyes

The meaning of eye movements is one of the most controversial aspects of NLP. The safest thing that can be said is that *some* people move their eyes in specific ways, according to the nature of the information they're processing. For example, lots of us raise our eyes heavenwards when someone surprises us with a tricky, embarrassing or (what appears to us) stupid question. But NLP goes a lot further.

Here is the standard NLP model for a right-handed person (for some left-handed people the pattern, it is said, may be reversed):

* Eyes up to their left: they're recalling something they've seen.
* Eyes up to their right: they're visualizing something they've never actually seen.
* Eyes horizontally across to their left: they're recalling a sound.
* Eyes horizontally across to their right: they're making up a sound (composing music, for example).
* Eyes down to their left: they're talking internally to themselves.
* Eyes down to their right: they're recalling a feeling.

If you'd like to test this out and come to your own conclusions then get some friends to be guinea pigs and ask questions designed to elicit the six different eye movements. For example, for visual recall, you might ask, 'Describe the view from your bedroom window', while for a feeling you might ask, 'Describe the sensation of diving into cold water.'

If you can identify these or other consistent eye patterns in a particular individual then you have a useful tool. On the basis of the NLP model, for example, if you asked somebody to describe where they were last night and you noted that their eyes flicked up to their right then you'd know they were making the whole thing up. However, various scientists have disputed that this pattern is common – let alone universal.

A very much more proven eye phenomenon is that of pupil size. Of course, pupils adapt to the light (and can be affected by drugs), but assuming stable lighting conditions, then dilation (enlargement) indicates pleasure. There's even a science known as 'pupillometrics', a term first used in 1975 by Eckhard Hess, a biopsychologist at the University of Chicago.

Most famously, the pupils of both men and women dilate when they're sexually attracted to someone. And, intriguingly, that dilation is itself attractive to the other person.

Controlling your own pupil dilation artificially isn't easy. If you're not attracted by someone else or deriving much pleasure from their company you could try thinking of something that does give you pleasure – pupils also dilate for good food, pets, landscapes and (in the case of women) babies.

Breathing

You can usually see when a person is breathing in and out by the rise and fall of the shoulders or chest and sometimes by the narrowing and flaring of the nostrils. Simply follow the same breathing pattern for rapport.

Congruence and lies

When well-balanced people are behaving naturally, they're congruent. That's to say, everything about them is harmonious. Every aspect of body language is in alignment and reflects their beliefs and values. But when somebody deliberately sets out to mislead or manipulate then – almost inevitably – there will be a degree of incongruence. One aspect of body language will contradict another. That's something you'll be looking for.

Dealing with inattention

People who are paying attention tend to be fairly still and ignore distractions. They lean forwards – perhaps with their heads slightly tilted – and gaze steadily with reduced blinking and maybe a furrowed brow. If they're open to what's being said their bodies are open (see below) and they may nod and make encouraging noises. It's easy to get in rapport with them. On the other hand, people who aren't interested tend to fidget, get distracted easily, look around for more interesting diversions and lean back. How you deal with that depends to a large extent on the context. A schoolmaster of mine used to throw pieces of chalk at pupils who had glazed over. More subtle devices include sudden changes of volume and rhythm and more energetic movements.

Dealing with closed attitudes

When people are open to others, to information and to experiences they literally tend to have 'open bodies'. That's to say, their hands will be open and their arms and legs will not be crossed. Clothing may also be open: jacket off, tie undone, shirt or blouse open at the neck. Note, however, that an open body can also denote aggression – come and get me if you dare. A closed body is the reverse; hands making fists, arms and legs crossed, shoulders hunched, head tucked down, are all signs that someone is shutting the world out. (But always bear in mind that these are also normal reactions to cold.)

In order to influence other people, you need to be able to get them out of closed postures into open postures. One way is to ask them to do something that requires them to use their hands. As a salesman you could, for example, pass out sample products. Another technique is to match their body language while you try to establish rapport in other ways. Once you have a connection, you then lead them into more open postures by opening your posture. If you've successfully initiated rapport they should follow your lead.

Submission and dominance

When someone is submissive the body is usually closed (see above), made as small as possible, and kept still, with the head down. In this mood people tend to smile a lot with the mouth but not with the eyes, which will be wide. Hands are often open, palms up, to show that there is no weapon. Movement is slow but jerky and there may be signs of tension such as sweating, a white face, pulling the hair and face touching.

By contrast, people who are feeling dominant make their bodies bigger, by pulling themselves up to their full height with arms held out and legs apart – which, by exposing the groin, is also a way for men to say 'mine is bigger than yours'. They may demonstrate their superiority by showing off expensive accessories (watches, cuff links, jewellery and so on), by 'invading' the territory of other people (getting very close, putting feet on the furniture) and interrupting or speaking over them. Dominant people tend not to worry about showing disapproval in their facial expressions.

Who dominates is something that tends to be established at the outset of a meeting. In the handshake, the dominant person aims to get his or her hand on top – not at the side – and will follow up with an elbow hold or a shoulder hold. They may either stare for a long time or, alternatively, quickly 'cut' the other person. Dominant people often use long silences when speaking, during which they look around at the people listening or stare off into space as they visualize their own importance.

You can rub along with dominant people simply by doing what they want – but that isn't the same as rapport. Indeed, it may be that rapport isn't actually possible. If you want to go for it, you'll simply have to rise to the challenge and match them.

Romance

It's not only birds and animals that preen and display. Humans do it too. Tossing the head, running fingers through hair, thrusting out breasts, holding in the stomach and holding out the arms to make the shoulders look bigger are all examples. Eyes are vitally important. From a distance someone may look for longer than normal, then look away, then back again. Close up, the pupils will be seen to be dilated (see *Eyes* above) when someone feels attracted. Eyes will also tend to go where a person would like to touch – for example, the lips or the groin. Most women will have had the experience of looking into the faces of men whose eyes keep darting down to their cleavage. People may unconsciously caress themselves in the way they'd like to caress the person they're interested in, or to be caressed by that person. The signal may also be given consciously. As rapport begins to develop, so people will automatically match one another – and again, this can be done consciously to try to create rapport.

Negotiations

What happens when one team of people goes to negotiate with another team? Let's say the directors of company A and the directors of company B. Without thinking, the company A directors will all sit on one side of the table and the company B directors will all sit on the opposite side. To most of us this feels so normal that we don't question it. But is it a good idea? It immediately creates an 'us and them' atmosphere. Sometimes that might be what you want but, for the purposes of conciliation, compromise and finding a win–win solution, it would actually be far better for 'opposite numbers' to sit next to one another. Thus the managing directors could sit side by side, the finance directors could sit side by side, and so on.

The Milton Model in everyday life

Largely by a process of observation, and by trial and error, Milton Erickson pioneered the techniques that were later modelled by Grinder and Bandler. Those techniques have now been studied and emulated by hypnotists and therapists all over the world. But many of them can also be used in everyday life and it's those we're going to look at here.

If you're a very direct sort of person, you may find it hard to adopt the Milton Model. Indeed, there are times when precision – the very opposite of the Milton Model – is essential. But we're not concerned here with something like flying an aeroplane. We're talking about changing the way people think and feel.

Using questions

Rather than giving instructions, which might meet with resistance, you can often get a better result by asking a question. For example, you might ask, 'How far are you willing to go?' By posing that question, you make it harder for the other person to say anything less than 'all the way'. And once they've said 'all the way' then they're committed.

Using negatives and positives

When people are feeling uncertain about something, it's important for rapport to show that you understand their negative feelings:

'I understand how you feel.'

'Everyone finds it difficult the first time.'

In fact, you can simply repeat back to people the negative things they've said: 'So you're saying you feel you're not ready to take this step...'. You can then overcome resistance by introducing negatives to discharge their feelings. For example, you might say:

'You don't have to continue if you're not enjoying it.'

'You won't have to sign anything.'

'You don't have to make a decision until you're completely convinced.'

Negatives, then, can be useful in certain situations. They can diffuse resistance. But when giving instructions, it's generally a very bad idea to phrase them in negative terms. So here's a very important lesson:

Always give instructions in positive terms.

Cause and effect

We're all used to statements which link a cause and an effect. You might say, for example: 'Prices are going up next month so it would be a good idea to order now.' The fact is, we're so used to them that any compound statement that begins with something obviously true tends to make us feel that the second part will also be right. The truth of the first part rubs off on the second:

'It's an unusually beautiful day so let's go to the beach.'

Put like that it seems such a natural thing to do (even if you should be at work). A variation is what's known as 'implication' using an 'if' construction:

'If you sit in that chair you'll feel more relaxed.'

The person who sits in the chair will generally follow their first positive response (sitting in the chair) with the second.

Pacing and leading

Pacing and leading together form a powerful technique in hypnosis but can also be used effectively on people in their normal waking state. Essentially, you feed their experience back to them (pacing) and once you've established rapport, you then guide them in the direction you want to go (leading). If you watch mentalists like Derren Brown and hypnotists like Paul McKenna on TV or YouTube you'll see them using this technique a lot.

Pacing can be:
* Physical – you match the other person's posture, mannerisms, tone of voice, breathing and so on.
* Verbal – you tell the other person the things they're experiencing at that moment.

This pacing not only creates rapport but also establishes a positive momentum which the other person may find hard to resist. Let's hear a good salesman in action: 'You have a very nice car there. It's a recent model with only 20,000 miles on the clock, and silver is a popular colour so in part-exchange I can offer you...'. The customer knows everything the salesman has said is true. It *is* a nice car, it *is* a recent model, it *is* low mileage and it *is* silver. So when the salesman makes a low offer the customer, carried along by the momentum, is inclined to accept.

Presuppositions and binds

The idea of presuppositions and binds is to make it necessary for the other person to summon up a certain strength of will to resist you. If they don't have that mental strength then you will persuade them.

Let's look at some simple presuppositions:
* 'Would you like to pay by credit card?'
* 'You've definitely chosen the best one.'
* 'You're so right to go for the pink.'

If these are said *before* any buying decision has actually been made then they have the effect of bumping the customer into doing what you want. Essentially, you're *presupposing* that they've decided to buy and they now have to actively resist you if they want to get out of the purchase.

Stories and quotes

It was probably his use of stories that was Erickson's most distinctive skill. People would come to him with a problem and, instead of doing anything about it (or so it appeared), he'd tell them a story. A few days or weeks later the problem would be gone.

Rather than say 'Do this' or 'Don't do that' (although he was also quite capable of giving orders when appropriate), Erickson would instead plant seeds that would sprout inside his clients' minds. The whole point of using stories, of course, is to go directly to the unconscious and bypass the resistance of the conscious mind. So the stories can't be too obvious.

If you've always been a fairly direct person, initially you'll struggle to come up with anecdotes that suit the circumstances. But if you work at it, over time you can build up your own personal 'library' and have an anecdote for every occasion. It will help if you think in terms of universal experiences, which could apply to just about everybody.

Phrasing

The pace at which you speak – and the way you separate groups of words by pauses – are crucial to your powers of persuasion. Most of us speak too quickly. If you think of the politicians whose words you give weight to (even if you don't necessarily agree), they'll probably be people who speak slowly and use plenty of pauses. Barack Obama immediately comes to mind. As we saw above, long pauses are a signal of dominance. And words delivered slowly give the impression of being well-considered and important, even if they're not. But there's another aspect to phrasing and that's its hypnotic effect. When you're up close to someone, attuning your speech to the rhythm of their breathing can be very powerful.

Compare this sentence with the first sentence of the above paragraph, for example:

> *The pace... at which you speak... and the way... you separate... groups of words... by pauses... are crucial... to your powers... of persuasion.*

Do you see the difference?

Motivation direction

We've already encountered motivation direction in Chapter 5, as it applies to you. It's what's known in NLP as a meta program and it applies equally to other people. Just to remind you, motivation direction is another way of saying 'stick or carrot'. Some people seem to respond more to sticks and some people more to carrots. NLP looks at this in terms of being motivated *away* from things that are negative and unpleasant, or being motivated *towards* things that are rewarding and enjoyable.

If you want to encourage somebody, you need to know their motivation direction. Generally speaking:

* 'Towards' people are fired up by goals and plans for the future and tend to be ambitious, energetic and optimistic. You motivate them using words such as: achieve, target, drive, reach, top and summit.
* 'Away from' people tend to be more aware of possible problems and are therefore more cautious. You motivate them using words such as: avoid, overcome, prevent, bunker and trap.

Using amnesia

Amnesia is a rather frightening word but, in fact, it simply means a loss of memory. Most people associate it with the word 'total' which, fortunately, is rare. Partial amnesia, on the other hand, is common.

Probably you've had the experience of someone suggesting an idea to you that, in fact, you had suggested to them a week or more previously. However much you protest, they insist it's their idea and say they have no memory of you ever having said any such thing. That's the frustrating side of partial amnesia. But you can also make the phenomenon work in your favour when you deliberately plant an idea that you *hope* another person will enthusiastically adopt as their own.

Partial amnesia can also work to your advantage when you don't want someone to think things over in case they change their mind or develop a resistance later.

Here, then, is a way of encouraging partial amnesia. Change the subject the *instant* you've planted your idea and then to talk about the new subject quickly, at length and in detail. The planted idea will remain in the unconscious but may be forgotten by the conscious mind.

transform your love life

Are you in love? Do you want to stay in love? Do you want to fall back in love? Do you want to increase the love you feel? Do you want to be a better lover? In this chapter we'll see how NLP can help you achieve all of these things.

8 transform your love life

Can you remember when you first met your partner? When you first began to get a special feeling? When you had your first kiss? When you first made love? When you made your first trip together? When you first moved in together?

When you think back on it, it's a movie, isn't it! A romantic story. Well, rather than watch television, why not lay back and, inside your head, run the movie in which *you* are one of the stars and *your partner* is the other! Let's call it *Love Story*. When you've finished watching it, feelings of love will overwhelm you.

Step 1: Select five very different romantic scenes from your life together with your partner.

Step 2: Acting like a film director, consider what qualities ('submodalities') you could change to maximize the romantic impact of each scene. There are all kinds of possibilities. For example, you can use several cameras from different viewpoints – or in NLP jargon, different 'perceptual positions'. You can show things through your own eyes at the time (first position), as well as through your partner's eyes (second position). And you can have yet another camera showing how you both would have looked to an observer (third position). Why not a slow motion sequence with some romantic music? How about a close-up for that first kiss? Maybe some soft-focus and low, mood lighting? And, of course, a bedroom scene. Nowadays, every romantic film has a bedroom scene. (We'll be having a look at that subject in more detail.)

Step 3: Once you're satisfied with your five scenes, run them one after the other to make your movie. Then run them all again a little faster. Then faster still.

Step 4: By now you should be overwhelmed by warm and loving feelings for your partner. Go and share them.

Running your very own romantic movie is something you should do regularly. Make a point of it at least once a week and your love will intensify.

To keep it interesting, vary the direction and as time moves on, you can add new scenes.

The Circle of Love

No matter how much you express your love for your partner, you can always express more. It's not just a case of what you *say* from time to time. Nor what you occasionally *give*. Nor what you *do* now and then. It's a question of feeling and radiating your love all the time you're together. This technique, which I call the Circle of Love, works on the same principles as the Circle of Confidence, with which you're already familiar.

Step 1: Search your memory for a past situation in which you felt overwhelmed by love. Relive that loving time, seeing and hearing everything in as much detail as possible. Particularly notice how you looked and how the love was oozing out of you. Accentuate the submodalities associated with love. Spin the feeling up.

Step 2: Imagine a circle on the floor. Take the love you felt on that previous occasion and pour it into the circle. Immediately the circle takes on a colour – the colour that, to you, is the colour of love. Maybe there's romantic music, too.

Step 3: Are there any other qualities you'll need? Maybe tenderness? Maybe empathy? If so, repeat the procedure, also pouring those qualities into your circle.

Step 4: Turn your thoughts to all those future occasions when you'll be wanting to feel those qualities. Select a cue. For example, it could simply be your partner arriving or it could be waking up next to him or her.

Step 5: Holding that cue in your mind, step into the circle and visualize all those qualities rising up from the floor, permeating you and being radiated by you.

Step 6: Future pace. Visualize the future unfolding from that cue moment. See yourself behaving with love and all the other qualities you've selected for your Circle of Love.

When the cue moment arrives for real, visualize the circle on the floor and step into it. Now express all that love to your partner.

The way we were

Sometimes it's a case of gradually drifting apart over months or years. And then there comes a point when you think of the way you *were* and want to get back to it once more.

By now you should be very familiar with the Swish concept – in effect, creating an emotion with one image and then quickly substituting a new image which acquires the same emotional charge as the first. Here we're going to use it to reawaken the feelings you used to have but which have now, perhaps, grown stale.

For the following Swish exercise, find yourself somewhere comfortable and quiet.

Step 1: Think of a time when you and your partner were deliriously happy together. From that period, select an image of your partner that made you overflow with love.

Step 2: Utterly revel in those loving feelings. Increase all the submodalities associated with love. Spin the feeling up to its maximum: see, hear, touch, taste and smell everything.

Step 3: Call up an image of your partner today and immediately Swish it into the place of the previous image, while retaining all the submodalities of the previous image and all the emotions.

Step 4: Repeat Steps 1–3 as many times as necessary, until those same loving feelings from years ago are firmly attached to your image of your partner today.

Dealing with rows

So you've had a row. The first thing you should do is recall the relevant NLP presupposition:

Underlying every behaviour is a positive intention.

Whatever it was you were arguing about, your partner had a positive intention in view and it would help to find out what that was.

When there's been a row, many people sulk and spontaneously use an NLP technique without knowing it — but to make the situation worse, not better. What a lot of us do is think of all the previous occasions when our partners have also done things that have upset us. We link them all together in a continuous movie and just make ourselves feel more and more resentful and annoyed. That's a very bad idea if you want the relationship to move forwards (but it's a very good idea when a relationship actually does end — see *Breaking up is not so hard to do*). Far better is to use the *Love Story* technique described above and run a 'movie' of all the good times.

Using different perspectives

When there's a disagreement, everyone's immediate reaction is to see a situation from their own point of view. That's perfectly normal. But you should never leave it at that. Always change perspective (see Chapter 2). In other words, imagine entering into your partner's body (second position) and seeing the situation from his or her perspective. Empathize; try to feel what he or she is feeling.

Next try third position. That's to say, imagine standing back from the pair of you so you can see not only your partner but also yourself. How do you look? Unreasonable, perhaps? Maybe slightly ridiculous? Even funny? If you were a third person, what would you do? Perhaps say, 'Come on you two, kiss and make up.'

Re-establishing rapport

After a row, you often seem to lose all rapport with your partner. Somehow you no longer seem able to tune in to one another's thoughts. Your movements are no longer synchronized. There's no symmetry. Everything jars. The complicity has gone.

One of the things you can do to help is deliberately use the matching and mirroring described in the previous chapter. Since your partner knows you very well it will have to be extremely subtle. On the other hand, if your partner notices then that just might be the moment to have a good laugh together.

The Romantic Behaviour Generator

This is an excellent way of installing a new behaviour. It can be used for everything – from being more empathetic to new lovemaking techniques. In this example, let's say you'd like to behave differently when criticized. At the moment your reaction is to withdraw love while you lick your wounds and think things over. You realize this makes the situation far worse then it need be, but you find it hard to change.

Step 1: Identify the old behaviour you would like to alter. In this example it's sulking.

Step 2: Identify the new behaviour you would like to have. For example, discussing the issue with good humour and without taking offence, so you both feel better afterwards.

Step 3: You are the director of a movie in which you are also the star. As the director, give instructions to yourself about the way you should behave. Watch yourself exhibit the new behaviour. In your role as director, make any corrections or changes you think necessary.

Step 4: Once you're satisfied, step into the movie and experience what it's like to have this new way of behaving, as seen through your own eyes as the star. Not only see but, of course, hear everything and feel what it's like. (In other words, you've now switched from third position to first position, that's to say, from dissociation to association.) Note the reaction of your partner. Is it what you want it to be?

Step 5: Move to second position. That's to say, see the whole scenario from your partner's viewpoint. Is it what your partner would want?

Step 6: Also check that this new behaviour really is suitable for you.

Step 7: If you're not happy with anything, return to your role as director, make the necessary changes and repeat Steps 3–6.

Step 8: Use future pacing. Visualize a situation in the future where you will want to behave in this new way. Look for a cue that could be used to trigger the behaviour automatically. In this example, it might be your partner looking angry, shouting or being tearful. Imagine yourself seeing or hearing the cue and immediately adopting the new behaviour. Play this 'film' as often as necessary until the new behaviour feels natural.

Step 9: Use the new behaviour in a real situation.

Improving your sex life

Anchors, as we've seen, are a normal part of our everyday experience and that includes our love lives. In fact, anchors are so much taken for granted when it comes to romance and sex that most people would probably find it hard to accept that they *are* anchors.

Take candles, for example. Most people would say that they're romantic – and low light does cause pupil dilation (see the previous chapter) – but otherwise there's nothing innately sexy about them. Before electricity, candles were just as normal as light bulbs are today. Nor is there anything innately romantic about champagne, nor oysters. But if you arrive home tonight and find a table lit by candles, champagne in an ice bucket and a plate of oysters then you'll probably feel very romantic indeed.

Discovering your partner's anchors

In a moment we'll be looking at how to create anchors for romance and sex. But before you do, it would be a good idea to discover your partner's existing anchors. He or she is bound to have quite a few – some entirely predictable and others much more personal that you might not know about.

With your partner, make a little game of it; each of you write down ten things that make you feel romantic and ten that make you feel aroused. Take turns guessing what your partner's anchors are. The one who gets the most correct is the winner (and the prize is up to you).

Establishing new anchors

In Chapter 5 we learned the NLP technique for setting anchors. When it comes to romance and sex, however, we can install them in a more natural way. As long as the same things are always followed by romance and (if you want) sex, then they will become anchors over time. The more often anchors are actually followed by romance (and sex), the more powerful they become. So it can be a good idea to have something of a routine. Not *everything* has to be routine, of course, just those certain elements.

Here are some suggestions:
* Kinaesthetic: the warmth of a log fire, nibbling an ear lobe, breathing in an ear, gently biting a tongue or lip while kissing, massaging the scalp or shoulders...
* Visual: a wink, an eyebrow raised in a particular way, a tongue run around the lips, special bed linen, a certain short skirt, certain underwear, stockings, a naked body...
* Olfactory: particular types of incense, perfume or aftershave...
* Gustatory: asparagus, oysters, a bottle of wine or champagne – but it has to be something special if it's to be an anchor, and served in a special way...
* Auditory: special pet names used only on romantic occasions, 'naughty' words, particular music only played for romantic occasions...

Adding erogenous zones

Given that the human body is fairly well endowed with sexual triggers is there really any point in creating more? Well, yes – a little variety in lovemaking technique is always good. And anyway, it's fun.

Here, then, is a way you can add to your partner's erogenous zones (or augment one that already exists). In effect, you'll be creating kinaesthetic anchors. You can also use the same procedure on yourself.

Have a go

Step 1: Identify the area you wish to 'erogenize'. It helps if it already has at least some special sensitivity.

Step 2: Stimulate your partner's most erogenous area until she or he is moderately excited.

Step 3: Stimulate the new area you wish to 'erogenize' with three caresses, slaps, scratches, nibbles or pinches (depending on what works best for that place).

Step 4: Immediately stimulate your partner's most erogenous zone again three times.

Step 5: Continue like this, alternating between the two areas, rhythmically stimulating each three times, until your partner reports that the new zone is beginning to generate sexual feelings.

The general tendency of lovers is either to go straight for the most erogenous zone or to work through the erogenous zones *in turn*, from the least to the most. It's because this technique *alternates* between the most erogenous area and a less erogenous area (or areas) that it has its special effect. In fact, over a lengthy session it's possible to erogenize the entire body in this way, at least for a while.

You can increase the effect by asking your partner to Swish images at the appropriate moments, first of all visualizing the most erogenous area and then abruptly substituting a visualization of the new area. The feelings associated with the first area will then become associated with the second.

Dealing with performance anxiety

Anxiety about sexual performance is fairly normal at the beginning of a relationship, but it can crop up at any time. When it does it can be fairly devastating because anxiety automatically leads to a reduction in blood flow where it's needed. Women can at least disguise it, but for men the effect is all too obvious. When you have a problem of this nature it's always best to discuss it with your partner. However, we'll assume here that you're tackling this on your own, at least for the moment. A simple visualization can help.

Step 1: In your mind's eye, see your partner preparing to have sex with you.

Step 2: Visualize the scene unfolding *very slowly*. Imagine yourself being completely relaxed as you see, hear, touch, taste and smell everything. See your partner becoming more and more aroused and see yourself responding just as you would wish to. Don't let any negative thoughts or doubts enter your mind while you're doing this.

Step 3: Adjust the submodalities to increase the impact. For example, you could zoom in on the details you find the most exciting or create multiple images.

Step 4: Play this visualization regularly to yourself and immediately before you make love.

You could also try setting anchors. As usual, it's best to have three different kinds of anchor – one visual, one auditory and one kinaesthetic. In this case, they'll all have to be under your control, both at the time of setting and at the time of firing.

Step 1: In your mind, see a previous occasion when you had amazing sex with your partner.

Step 2: Build your excitement (you can stimulate yourself physically as well as mentally, if you wish).

Step 3: Just *before* your excitement reaches a peak, set your anchors.

Step 4: Create a break state by thinking of something completely non-sexual.

Step 5: Repeat Steps 1–4 as many times as you feel necessary.

Step 6: Fire the anchors to see what happens. If you become aroused then it's worked. If not, go through the procedure again and again on other days.

Step 7: Once the anchors are established, future pace by visualizing scenes in which you successfully fire your anchors with your partner.

Step 8: Have sex with your partner using the anchors.

Self-hypnosis for performance anxiety

The Betty Erickson self-hypnosis method can also be used to help you overcome performance anxiety and make love more confidently and successfully. If you've forgotten how to put yourself into a trance, refer back to Chapter 1. When you're stating the purpose of your self-hypnosis (Step 3), say something like: 'I am entering into a trance for the purpose of allowing my unconscious mind to make the adjustments that will help me feel more confident in my lovemaking.' When you come to the visualization (Steps 5f and 5g), imagine a scene in which you are behaving in the way you want.

Breaking up is not so hard to do

NLP can help you improve your relationship and stay together, but there's absolutely no point using NLP or anything else to try to convince yourself that incompatibility is a fine basis for a relationship. Some relationships must come to an end and, when they do, one partner is often unable to accept the situation.

What should you do if you've been 'dumped' and can't get over it? Here's a technique that can help. It's the opposite of the *Love Story* technique described above. I call it the *Goodbye Story*.

Step 1: Instead of making yourself miserable by thinking about all the nice things associated with the person who dumped you, think instead of the *bad* things. There must have been some. Think of how your partner looked first thing in the morning. Think of your ex's worst physical aspects: the rolls of fat, the wrinkles round the neck, the sagging flesh, whatever it might be. Think of the times your partner let you down. Think of the worst thing your partner ever did to you. Carry on until you have five 'Worst Of' memories.

Step 2: Analyse each of the five scenes like a film director. What things could you do to increase their impact? Experiment with the submodalities. Maybe a close-up of the bags under the eyes? Maybe louder volume for that row? Maybe some soundtrack music that you hate? Really put time and effort into this. Experience each scene to the maximum.

Step 3: Once you're satisfied with your five scenes, make them into a movie by running them one after another without a break. Then run the whole movie again a bit faster. Then run it faster still. Then yet again.

Step 4: Future pace. Visualize meeting your ex and feeling *nothing*. Certainly not love or desire, but not anger or hatred either. Having overcome a break-up in this way doesn't mean you have to be vindictive. In fact, you'll probably feel a lot more reasonable as you begin to feel less emotional. If you no longer care very much, then you've succeeded. Otherwise repeat the whole exercise on a daily basis until you're 'cured'.

Notes

Notes

Sile
Barton
Son / Autistic